The Intuitive Artichoke
A Year of Meatless Mondays

Recipes: Vicky Gosse
Recipe Photos: Georgia Gosse

DEDICATION

For Dwayne, the love of my life, and Zach and Georgia, you have my heart. I love you.

eat the rainbow!

xoxo Vicky

FORWARD

My intention with this cookbook is to make vegetables and vegetarian cooking easy, accessible and enjoyable. I use ingredients that are in the pantry or at the produce section of the local grocery store. Organic local is always my first choice but please do what's right for you. There are the dirty dozen that are the main ones to eat organic (strawberries, spinach, nectarines, apples, peaches, pears, cherries, grapes, celery, tomatoes, sweet bell peppers and potatoes) and then there are the clean fifteen that don't need to be (corn, avocado, pineapple, cabbage, onion, peas, papaya, asparagus, mango, eggplant, honeydew, kiwi, cantaloupe, cauliflower and grapefruit).

This book was a long time coming. I first started writing a cookbook years ago at the urging of friends. I puttered around with it for a bit then let it go.
I love developing new recipes and always have. I see a beautiful or unusual vegetable and try to figure out what to do with it. Eating out or other people's food inspires me to recreate it to my own taste. I like to take family recipes and reconstruct them into vegetarian so they still have that familiar flavour profile.

Meatless Monday came about when my sister, Candace McKim -Yogini's Guide, asked me to be a contributor to her weekly newsletter. After a year I realized that I had a book! Presto! Instant (not really) cookbook.

I really want to take the scary weird vibe out of vegetarianism and encourage everyone to go meatless one day a week. A day that is looked forward to as yummy, fun and exciting! Delight in the culinary adventure!

ACKNOWLEDGMENTS

I would like to acknowledge the help and guidance of my sister, Candace McKim in the creation of my cookbook. I started playing around with vegetarian cooking because she didn't eat meat, but still wanted to be a part of family meals and celebrations. Flying by the seat of my pants, I reworked favourite flavour profiles into new dishes. When her book launched, there were such lackluster catering options that I did it myself.

Shortly thereafter, I started doing a Meatless Monday offering on her newsletter, which has translated into this book. Thank you Candace, your perception, intuition and creativity catapulted me somewhere I didn't know I could go.

I am grateful to my daughter, Georgia Gosse, for her brilliant photos and ruthlessly honest opinions. She is frequently asked to drop everything to dash outside to take a photo. Zachary Gosse, my son, is a true foodie and shares his knowledge about all the latest trends and techniques. He has a business brain and has lots of ideas for me.

I would like to thank my husband, Dwayne Gosse for being open to many different food experiments and gamely trying them. All he wants is for me to be happy, however that looks. He is endlessly patient listening to my hopes and dreams, anxieties and irritations.

My extended family have a standing invitation to Sunday dinners and are excellent guinea pigs. I once painstakingly marinated, roasted and grilled a whole carrot for my niece, Chloe Mckim, as a hot dog replacement. Epic fail!!! They are all so loving and supportive, I'm not afraid to try something new that isn't guaranteed to work.

My best friend, Cathi Armitstead, treats me with such respect and admiration that I strive to live up to her opinion. She makes me laugh and is awesome at cleaning up after my culinary tornadoes.

My parents Joyce and Garth Bertrand have encouraged me my entire life and although "simple is best", they are always ready to try anything!

I acknowledge with gratitude all the love from so many, as well as the amazing opportunities that come my way. I love you all so much. Thank you!

Let's Eat!!!

~ Vicky

DISCLAIMER

The recipes in this book have been carefully tested by our kitchen. To the best of our knowledge they are safe and nutritious for ordinary use and users. For those people with food or other allergies or who have special food requirements or health issues please read the contents of each recipe carefully and determine whether or not they may create a problem for you. All recipes are used at the risk of the consumer. We cannot be responsible for any hazards, loss or damage that may occur as a result of any recipes. For those with special needs, allergies, requirements or health problems, in the event of any doubt, please contact your medical advisor prior to the use of any recipe.

The Intuitive Artichoke

TABLE OF CONTENTS

SUNRISE
EATS

SUNRISE EATS

For me, breakfast needs to be quick, tasty and in my hand. Brunch, on the other hand, can be quite wonderful as it slows down, and often contains booze.

For meatless Mondays, or any day when you are choosing a vegetarian breakfast, eggs are your friend. Apart from the ubiquitous omelet, poached, fried, or scrambled eggs, I have gathered a few recipes that vegetarians and vegans relish. Breakfast for dinner is often a go to in our busy household. Applause!

Hey! The 80's called! They love the new hipster brunch potato skins!!

AVOCADO AND EGG STUFFED SWEET POTATO
2 sweet potatoes scrubbed and halved lengthwise
2 tablespoons olive oil
4 extra large eggs
Shredded cheese
1 avocado diced fine
4 tablespoons salsa
Salt and pepper to taste
Cilantro chopped (to garnish)

Caress sweet potatoes with olive oil and bake at 375 degrees for 40 minutes or until soft. Scoop out inside of potato leaving a half-inch shell. Crack one egg into each potato shell, sprinkle with salt, pepper and cheese. Bake 15-20 minutes until egg is at desired doneness. Top with diced avocado, salsa and cilantro.

A luscious creamy frittata bursting with fresh garden flavours of tomato and zucchini with the nice warm hum of chilies.

ZINGY ZUCCHINI FRITATTA
2 tablespoons olive oil
One bunch green onions diced
Two small zucchini diced
1 tin mild green chilies
Half pint grape tomatoes halved
1/4 cup parsley chopped
Salt and pepper to taste

8 eggs - beaten with
1/2 cup plain Greek yogurt
1/2 cup milk
2 tablespoons sriracha
1/4 - 1/2 teaspoon cayenne
Salt and pepper to taste

11/2 - 2 cups shredded cheese (meltable)

In 10" skillet sauté vegetables in olive oil over medium low heat. Add in egg mixture. Slowly fold in cheese. Cook until edges set and slight wobble in middle. Place under broiler until golden on top. Cut into wedges and serve with chunks of dark crusty seed bread. Fantastic paired with Fennel Walnut Salad.

FIFTY SHADES OF AVOCADO TOAST

The crunchy sourness of San Francisco's finest yeasty offering cradles the voluptuous velvet of luscious avocado, achingly caressed by salt and slapped (hurts so good!) with the sting of lime. If your safe word is "go" - try green onion, cilantro, jack cheese, salsa, egg, caviar, pine nuts, pumpkin seeds, sweet potato, potato chips, sour cream, lemon juice, orange segments, cinnamon, tostado, rice cake, garlic, jalapeño peppers, dried chili flakes, hemp seeds, chia seeds, flax seeds, sunflower seeds, cumin, feta, blueberries, corn chips, nachos, banana chips, pita bread, multigrain bread, bagels, olives, capers, sun-dried tomatoes, banana peppers, vegetarian crumble, tomatoes, lettuce, cucumber, white bean purée, hot sauce, toasted coconut, seasoning salt, quinoa, mint, honey, pineapple, spinach, popcorn, chipotle, carrot, radish, mango, chives....

AVOCADO ON TOAST

2 slices sour dough bread
1 avocado mashed
1/2 lime juiced
Himalayan pink sea salt

Toast bread. Mashed together avocado, lime juice and salt. Divide and pile high on toast. Delicious as is or add any toppings or bottoms you choose. You're limited only by your imagination

Shivery and ebullient - ice cream for breakfast? And oh! So pretty!

SMOOTHIE BOWL
3 cups frozen mixed berries
1 scoop Vega One vanilla protein powder (or your favourite)
1 lime juiced
1 orange juiced
1/2 cup water, almond milk, coconut milk or pomegranate juice

Blitz all together in a blender, food processor, vita mix, or with your immersion blender. Consistency should be thick like pudding. Add more liquid if necessary.

Toppings
pumpkin seeds
raspberries
blackberries
granola

Note: if you want to make a smoothie add extra liquid for a sippable consistency.

Deceptively healthy this breakfast beauty is discipline spanked by flavour!!

TOFU SCRAMBLE
1 block extra firm or pressed tofu
1 teaspoon olive oil or vegan margarine
1/2 onion diced
1 clove garlic minced
2 tablespoons nutritional yeast
1/2 teaspoon each turmeric, cumin, paprika
1 cup assorted mushrooms diced
1 bell pepper diced
2 links vegan chorizo sausage
2 avocados sliced in half, pit removed

Drain tofu between two layers of kitchen towel with a weight on top. Heat oil in a large skillet and cook onion and garlic until fragrant. Crumble in the tofu and sprinkle with spices. Toss in the veggies and spicy sausage, stirring to combine. Keep cooking until veg is soft, adding a scant splash of water if needed. Taste for seasoning and grind in pepper and sea salt to taste. Lavish over avocado and savour with whole grain toast! It's exquisite as is or divine topped with (vegan) cheese, sour cream, salsa, and/or cilantro. Serve with spiced oranges.

This charming temptress always delights! Mellow yet ambrosial - she'll try anything!

SPICED ORANGES
4 oranges
1/4 teaspoon each cayenne, sugar, salt, lime zest
1 tablespoon lime juice
Peel whole oranges. Spritz on lime juice and sprinkle with spice mixture.

Sweet potato toast - Shockingly satisfying, this sweet tuber is an earthy, exotic vehicle.

SWEET POTATO TOAST
1 sweet Potato scrubbed or peeled

Cut sweet potato into 1/4 inch slices. Pop into toaster and toast. Again. And again. And once more with feeling! I like mine brown and blistered so I do it again, but it depends on your toaster and your taste buds.
Top your toast anyway you like. Nut butter with smashed bananas or berries. Avocado and its many friends. Tofu or egg scramble. Roasted vegetables. Lettuce, tomato, vegan cheese and veganaise. Tapenade. Dark chocolate and marshmallow. Colour outside the lines!
Sweet Potato Toast will keep a few days in the fridge and can be re-toasted.

NOTES:

Vicky Gosse

SULTRY
SOUPS

SULTRY SOUPS

Mmmm! Hot soup on a cold day... So comforting, like a hug from grandma. Cold soup is especially refreshing on a hot day. Soup can be used to start a meal, it can be a meal, and it is my favourite medicine. Soup is also great as an appy in a little shot glass.

I always like to make the new and unusual that no one has tried, that way they have no frame of reference! Studies have shown that you can drink a glass of water and eat a salad, or cook the salad in the same amount of water and feel satisfied longer eating less.

Soup can be quick and easy to make which means it's a great choice for busy days. Almost any of your favourite dishes can be made into soup. You can eat soup every day for a year and not have the same exact soup twice. Think about a dish and what goes into it and you have your desired taste. With vegetarian broth being super simple to make or buy, and coconut milk readily available it's a cinch!

Ooh La La!! Rich caramelized onions simmered in wine. Deux pour la soupe et deux pour moi.

VEGETARIAN FRENCH ONION SOUP
4 large onions quartered and sliced
1/4 cup butter
1/4 cup olive oil
2 teaspoon soy sauce
Cracked pepper to taste
2 cloves garlic minced
8 sprigs fresh thyme or 1 teaspoon dried
1 litre vegetable stock
2 tablespoons vegetable or mushroom Better Than Bouillon
2 cups red wine or 2 cups stock
1 cup water

Four slices of French bread toasted
1 cup grated Swiss divided onto toast
1 bunch green onion to garnish

In large Dutch oven caramelize onions in butter and oil until golden. Low & slow for 45 minutes. Stir in rest of ingredients and simmer to cook off alcohol. Remove thyme sprigs and divide into four bowls. Top with toast and cheese and broil. Garnish with green onion. Fantastic with Arugula Pear salad.

When you're exhausted and can't even - a sweet and spicy, savory squash soup. Flavour bomb!!

BUTTERNUT SQUASH SOUP
2 tablespoons butter
½ cup frozen diced onion
2 tablespoons ginger grated
1 tablespoon garlic minced
¼ teaspoon cinnamon
¼ teaspoon nutmeg
¼ teaspoon cayenne pepper
1 teaspoon Himalayan sea salt
1 litre vegetarian broth
1 package frozen butternut squash
1 cup unsweetened applesauce
½ cup pumpkin seeds to garnish

Giant glass of your favourite wine

In a large pot, sauté the onion in butter. Throw in seasonings, broth, squash, and heat through. Blitz with stick blender (or in a jug blender in batches) until smooth. Garnish with applesauce and pumpkin seeds.

Put up your feet and enjoy your wine. You are SUPERWOMAN!!!

'mato Soup - all grown up!! Basil tries to get fresh with a tomato, but gin is the panty remover!

TOMATO BASIL SOUP WITH GIN
2 tablespoons basil infused olive (or add 1 teaspoon dried basil to olive oil)
½ cup onion (diced)
3 cloves garlic (grated fine)
2 bay leaves
Salt and pepper
3 cups vegetable broth
3 tins diced tomatoes (14 oz. each)
¼ cup gin
1 teaspoon pepper
2 teaspoon Himalayan pink sea salt (to taste)
2 cup basil (finely shredded)

In a Dutch oven heat oil and sauté onion, garlic and bay leaves with salt and pepper. Pour in broth, tomatoes and gin. Season to taste and simmer 20 minutes. Remove bay leaves and blend soup in batches or with an immersion blender. Add in fragrant basil. Sublime!! Check seasonings and adjust. (Salt will vary widely depending on levels of salinity in broth and tomatoes.)
*You can substitute vodka instead of gin.

The soothing serenity of Zen-like zucchini is craaazy with curry!

ZUCCHINI GAZPACHO
1 tablespoon olive oil
1 medium onion, chopped
Himalayan pink sea salt
2 cloves garlic minced
3 teaspoons curry powder
3 medium zucchinis sliced 1 inch chunks
1 large potato sliced into 1 inch chunks
1 litre vegetable stock
1/4 cup toasted flaked almonds to garnish

In a large skillet heat oil and cook onion with salt until soft. Sprinkle in curry and garlic, stir continuously one minute until fragrant. Simmer potatoes in stock for ten minutes, add zucchini and simmer for another 10 minutes, flavour with spicy onion mix. Puree with an immersion blender or in a blender in batches until smooth. Chill in fridge. Over a medium heat lightly toast almonds. Watch carefully so they don't burn! Garnish soup. I like to serve in small glasses.

Earthy, savory and filling. Warms the cockles when its blustery and doesn't heat up the house on a hot summer day.

LENTIL SPINACH SOUP
2 cups lentils
8 cups vegetable stock
1 medium onion diced small
1 cup celery diced small
1 tablespoon Greek seasoning
1 teaspoon dried thyme
2 teaspoons dried oregano
4 cloves minced garlic
Fresh ground black pepper to taste
1 28oz tin diced tomatoes
1 large bunch spinach washed and chopped
1 lemon squeezed over soup
Feta crumbled garnish if desired

Combine all ingredients (except spinach, lemon and feta) in crockpot. Cook on low 6-8 hours or on high 4-5 hours. Taste, adjust seasonings and add spinach thirty minutes before serving. Spritz with lemon. Feta cheese can be served on top as a salty garnish. Everything can be made in the crockpot the night before and switched on in the morning.
*Salt varies wildly depending on the sodium content of veg stock and tomatoes. Always taste for desired seasoning.

There's no way to make this sound seductive. It's warm, hearty, low cal with lots of veg. Awesome to sip on while trying to figure out dinner, as a snack, or when you're under the weather. Light and filling - you feel snug - so thats kinda sexy?

CABBAGE SOUP
½ head of cabbage chopped fine
1/2 cup each celery, onion, carrots diced
1 bell pepper, diced
2 tablespoons olive oil
3 cloves garlic minced
4 cups vegetable broth
28 oz tin diced tomatoes
1 teaspoon dried oregano
2 teaspoons dried basil
2 bay leaves
2 teaspoons turmeric
½ teaspoon red pepper flakes
Himalayan pink sea salt and pepper
1/2 lemon or lime juiced

Heat olive oil in a large pot and gently sauté celery, onions, bell peppers, and carrots. Stir in garlic. Quickly pour in broth, tomatoes and cabbage, bring to a boil and reduce heat. Add in oregano, basil, red pepper flakes, pepper and salt. Cook until cabbage is tender and taste broth. Adjust seasoning if needed. Spritz with a sparky citrus blast.
This is the basic recipe but feel free to change it up with different broths, vegetables, herbs and spices. Throw rice, noodles, potato or quinoa into individual bowls for a carby boost!

Here comes the sun! Creamy and flavourful, brimming with good for you, miracle spice turmeric! The bland silkiness of cauliflower purée is the perfect foil to showcase the golden beauty.

TURMERIC CAULIFLOWER SOUP
2 tablespoons EVOO
1 medium onion diced
2 tablespoons turmeric
1 tablespoon cumin
1/2 teaspoon dried red chilies
2 cloves minced garlic
One large head cauliflower chopped
1 litre vegetable broth
1 tin coconut milk
Himalayan pink sea salt and fresh cracked black pepper to taste
4 tablespoons chopped nuts

In a large pot sauté onion in hot oil and sprinkle with spices to toast until fragrant. Briefly cook garlic to soften as well. Dump in cauliflower and broth, cook until tender. Pour in the coconut milk and purée with an immersion blender. Adjust seasonings adding Himalayan pink sea salt and fresh cracked black pepper as needed. Divide into four bowls and garnish with chopped nuts.

NOTES:

Vicky Gosse

SAVOURY

SALADS

27

SAVOURY SALADS

Salads are a virtuous way of eating what you feel like! They were at one point iceberg lettuce, a few vegetables and bottled dressing. Now they can be an entire meal. Up the protein content by adding beans, legumes, nuts, seeds and quinoa. Ramp up the fiber and satiety with the addition of grains like barley, amaranth or brown rice.

We can crunch down on our cruciferous veg and release tension, we can eat our spinach and instantly feel strong, we can order a salad at a restaurant and feel like we're doing something good for our bodies.

Salads are an awesome way to add greens to your day, to eat a colourful array of produce, get extra water into your diet and to try something new. A basic rule of thumb is that if it grows together, it goes together!
Try out these recipes and change them up to suit your yourself.

Dressings are techniques that can be altered as well. Different types and flavours of oil and vinegars, spices and herbs. Fling caution to the wind and challenge your taste buds.

Apres divorce perfection! The peppery bitterness of the arugula is perfectly offset by the luscious pear with nuts on your plate - where they belong.

ARUGULA PEAR SALAD
4 loose handfuls of arugula
1 pear or apple sliced thin with mandolin or vegetable peeler
1/2 c toasted pecans
Vinaigrette
Whisk together;
1/3 c apple cider vinegar
1 tablespoon Dijon
1/3 cup extra virgin olive oil

Arrange arugula on 4 plates. Top with sliced fruit and nuts.
Dribble vinaigrette over.
C'est magnifique!

Fantastic with French Onion Soup.

The crunch of cool iceberg sparked with a lively bite of anise.

FENNEL WALNUT SALAD
6 c shredded iceberg lettuce
2 bulbs fennel - finely shaved
1/3 c walnuts - chopped and toasted
2 lemons - juiced
1/4 c. Extra virgin olive oil
Pink Himalayan sea salt

Mound lettuce on plate and shave fennel over. Top with walnuts, sprinkle with lemon, drizzle EVOO over and finish with a few grinds of salt.

Mmmmmmm!

First class alongside Zucchini Frittata.

All hail mighty Caesar, vegetarians rejoice!
Barbecues are safe again!!!

GRILLED CAESAR SALAD
Two small heads Romaine lettuce
Caesar Salad Dressing *most dressings contain anchovies
Parmigiana Reggiano cheese
Fresh ground pepper
Lemon (wedges)
4 baguette slices toasted

DRESSING
1/4 cup hummus
1 teaspoon Dijon mustard
1/2 teaspoon lemon zest
1 lemon juiced
2 tablespoons capers with juice chopped
5 cloves garlic rasped or minced
1 tablespoon nutritional yeast or pinch of sea salt
2 tablespoons olive oil
Fresh ground pepper to taste

Mix in a bowl, thinning with hot water if needed.

Carefully wash and cut each head of lettuce in half, leaving
core intact. (If heads are large cut into quarters.) Brush
each cut side of Romaine generously with your Caesar
dressing. Grill until lettuce is slightly wilted, and has
delicious crispy bits and char marks. Top with Parmigiana
Reggiano and a squeeze of lemon. A slice of crispy
baguette toast is astounding to sop up all the leftover
dressing.

Charred asparagus gets all hot and bothered by the briny embrace of feta. Lemons' astringent bite completes this ménage a trois.

WARM ASPARAGUS SALAD
Large bunch asparagus
2 tablespoon Olive Oil
2 lemons (halved)
½ teaspoon fresh ground pepper
½ teaspoon Himalayan sea salt
½ cup feta cheese
Pita

In a large bowl lovingly toss asparagus with oil, salt, pepper and lemon halves. Grill on the barbecue until asparagus is tender, crisp, and lemons are charred. Divide evenly onto plates. Top with feta and squeeze scorched lemons all over.

Loves to frolic with roasted potatoes!

Salty with a briny tang - crisp yet pungent - and a sweetly acidic burst! Add in a garlicky Tzatziki and mop it all up with pita. Oh! Those Greeks!!!

GREEK SALAD
2-3 cups cherry tomatoes
2-3 cups cucumber bite sized chunks
1 cup feta bite sized chunks
1 cup Kalamata olives
½ cup red onion bite sized chunks
1/3 cup loosely packed fresh oregano
1/3 cup EVOO
1/3 cup vinegar balsamic or red wine
Fresh cracked black pepper to taste

Toss all together in an enormous bowl to mix thoroughly. Season with pepper and enjoy!

Beauteous babe Barb makes this bodacious badass
bean salad bursting with broccoli. Bountiful enough to
feed all your brawny bro's and bewitching bitches!!!

BEAN SALAD
1 tin each of red kidney beans, white kidney beans,
Romano beans, black beans, garbanzo beans, wax beans
and green beans (rinsed and drained)
1 of each red, orange, yellow and green pepper 1/2 inch
chunks
1 tin baby corn rinsed and drained
4 cups broccoli small florets and sliced stalk
1 bunch red radish sliced
1 bunch green onion sliced
1 cup balsamic vinegar fig is yummy
½ cup extra virgin olive oil
½ teaspoon garlic purée
Himalayan sea salt and fresh cracked pepper to taste

1 bunch parsley chopped
1 English cucumber peeked into ribbons

In an enormous bowl mix together beans, peppers and
vegetables. Dress with oil, vinegar and garlic paste. Grind
over the salt and pepper. Marinate for 6-24 hours. Half an
hour before serving, spatter with parsley. Strew cucumber
over individual servings. Perfect for potluck or barbecue.
Keeps for days, getting better and better!

70's Psychedelic coleslaw - a far out cosmic kaleidoscope of crunch and colour, man. Trippy tahini dressing makes love not war to the chomp of cabbage and carrots. Peace baby.

PSYCHADELIC COLESLAW
1/3 purple cabbage shredded
1 each yellow and orange pepper sliced thin
1/2 medium sweet onion sliced thin
2 inch chunk ginger finely grated
2 raw beets coarsely grated or use spiralizer
3 raw carrots coarsely grated or use spiralizer
1 cup cilantro chopped or parsley if cilantro tastes like soap to you

DRESSING
1/2 cup tahini
1/4 cup rice wine vinegar
2 limes juiced, 3 tablespoons juice
2 tablespoon maple syrup
1 teaspoon hot sauce
1 teaspoon powdered ginger
Warm water as needed

Sling together ginger with cabbage, pepper and onion. Artfully tangle the spiralized veg on top. Strew chopped cilantro with abandon. Dress slaw with tahini et al (shaken together) at last minute to prevent the aggressive purplish colour taking over. Leftovers are surprisingly tasty added to a stir fry!

Nestle edamame between crunchy celery and juicy tomatoes, stud with jewels of red pepper. The unctuous feta is turned on by the throaty salinity of Kalamata olives. Soothe the crunch with rich velvety avocado dressing.

EDAMAME MASON JAR SALAD
1 1/2 cup shredded zucchini
1/2 cup celery sliced diced
1/2 cup edamame
1/2 cup cherry tomatoes
1/2 cup red pepper diced
1/2 cup kalamata olives
1/2 cup feta cheese

AVOCADO DRESSING
1 large avocado
1 lemon juiced
1/2 cup spinach
3 tablespoons olive oil
Himalayan pink sea salt
Fresh ground pepper

Whiz together in a blender

Assemble in two 1 litre mason jars, divide and layer dressing, celery, tomatoes, edamame, peppers, olives, feta and stuff in zucchini.
This will easily keep in the fridge for 5 days or more. Just dump into a big bowl and enjoy!

Belly up to the happy beet beat. The funky crunch of cauliflower rice is uplifted by zucchinis Zen. Rain down carrot confetti and pomegranate pearls. The bed of quinoa is blanketed with a spinach duvet. Bring it all together with a luscious tahini dressing.

CAULIFLOWER RICE BUDDHA BOWL
2 cups cooked quinoa
4 cups spinach (lightly sautéed)
2 cups cauliflower (riced on a box grater)
4 carrots thinly sliced (mandolin-medallion sized)
2 medium zucchini thinly sliced (spiralized or mandolined)
1 cup green lentils cooked
4 small beets thinly sliced (spiralized or grated)

Divide and assemble into four bowls. Top with tahini dressing.

TAHINI DRESSING
1/2 cup tahini (sesame paste)
1/4 cup olive oil
1/4 water
2 tablespoons tamari or soy sauce
1/4 red wine vinegar
1/2 lemon (juiced)
2 inch chunk grated ginger
Fresh ground black pepper to taste

Blend all together until smooth. Pour over Buddha Bowls.

Simple, satisfying yet sumptuous. With ingredients this gorgeous you need only to enhance their naked beauty.

FARMERS MARKET TOMATO SALAD
Tomatoes - the best you can find or grow - lots of colours and variety
Grey fleur de sel - to taste
Fresh basil - torn roughly to release perfume
Extra Virgin Olive Oil - to drizzle

Slice large heirloom tomatoes and make a bed on your prettiest plate. Cut medium sized tomatoes into chunks and decorate on top. Mound grape tomatoes in the centre. Artfully strew with basil, freckle on the salt and weep olive oil over all. Have plenty of good crusty bread to soak up all those delicious flavours.

Garlicky and cheesey, orzo is the perfect vessel for this rustic pasta salad. The fresh herbs elevate to elegant extravagance.

ORZO SALAD WITH FRESH HERBS
1 package dried orzo cooked in vegetable stock
1/2 cup olive oil
2 cloves garlic minced
2 lemons zested and juiced
1 cup fresh grated parmesan cheese
1 cup fresh chopped herbs (mix of parsley, basil and cilantro with small amounts of rosemary, chives, sage, thyme)
Fresh cracked pepper - lots!
Good quality sea salt to taste
1 pint grape tomatoes - halved

Cook orzo according to package directions. Spread onto cookie sheet to stop cooking and cool quickly. Drizzle with EVOO and lemon juice. Sprinkle garlic, zest and parmesan cheese. Stir in herbs and lots of pepper. Taste and add more pepper and salt if necessary. Dust tomatoes with salt and pile up in the middle of salad. Scrumpy served warm or room temperature. I enjoy the leftovers heated.

Crisply fresh and satiating. The toothsome mango perfectly heightens the resinous nut, the puritanical legume, and the verdant foliate.

MANGO MASON JAR SALAD
1/3 cup mango dressing
Cooked brown rice
Cooked lentils and black beans
Cooked butternut squash cubes
Cucumber chunks
Diced green onion
Pine nuts (lightly toasted)
1 mango sliced and diced
Spinach (packed tightly)

Layer ingredients (in a1litre mason jar) in order. Amounts will vary according to taste. Store in fridge up to five days. Just tip into a large bowl and toss to enjoy.

MANGO DRESSING
1 mango, peeled, pitted and roughly chopped
2 limes juiced
2 tablespoons maple syrup
½ teaspoon cumin
2 inch chunk ginger grated
1 clove garlic minced
⅓ cup extra virgin olive oil
1/2 - 1 finely chopped jalapeño (depending on how spicy you like things.)
Himalayan pink sea salt to taste
Whiz it all together in a blender until smooth and creamy, adding a little water or orange juice to thin. Taste and add salt and more jalapeno if necessary. Dressing will make 4 salads.

The robust green of kale is tempered by salty, bitter celery and the tart sweetness of apple.

KALE CRUNCH SALAD
1 head kale torn into bite-sized pieces
1 head celery sliced thin (stalks and leaves)
1 apple sliced very thin (spritz with lemon)
1/2 jicama (apple sized) sliced into very thin strips

Massage dressing into the kale and sprinkle with Himalayan sea salt. Toss all ingredients together.

BALSAMIC VINAGRETTE
1/3 cup balsamic vinegar
1 teaspoon mustard
Himalayan pink sea salt
Fresh ground pepper
1/3 cup extra virgin olive oil
Vigorously shake all ingredients together in a jar. Extra dressing will keep in the fridge Let sit on the counter for half an hour before serving so the EVOO goes back to a liquid state.

There is something so inviting about a big bowl of life-giving, colourful veggies. Ancient grains add a nutty, satisfying comfort and seeds provide a munchy nibble. Balance all this celestial clean-living with decadent desert, or a big glass of wine!

BUILD A BETTER BUDDHA BOWL
1 large carrot, sliced
1 tin chickpeas, sautéed with a sprinkle of cumin, turmeric, and cayenne
1 cup fresh green beans, topped and tailed, cut into bite sized pieces
2 cups faro, cooked as per package instructions
1 red pepper, cut into strips
2 cups cooked cabbage
4 cups romaine lettuce torn
1/2 cup pumpkin seeds

In 4 large bowls arrange in an aesthetically pleasing manner. Top with dressing.
Buddha bowls are a grain, a green, a veg, and a bean. Add nuts or seeds, and a yummy dressing.

SWEET AND SPICY DRESSING
1/2 cup white balsamic vinegar
1/4 cup marmalade or peach jam
1/4 teaspoon dried chilies
1/2 cup extra virgin olive oil
Vigorously shake together vinegar, jam and chilies. When combined whisk in olive oil. Season with Himalayan pink sea salt and fresh cracked pepper.

A diverse, three dimensional depiction of early 20th century avant-garde salad from multiple viewpoints. Eden's original-sin fruit seduces sweet and tart, exotic chayote excites and kohlrabi kicks ass!!!

CUBIST SALAD
2 large juicy crisp apples cubed
2 chayote squash peeled, seeded and cubed
2 bulbs of kohlrabi peeled and cubed
2 stalks celery cubed
2 lemons juiced
1/3 cup extra virgin olive oil
4 large handfuls of arugula
Himalayan pink sea salt

Spritz freshly chopped apples with lemon to prevent browning. Combine cubed fruit and vegetables in a large bowl. Shake lemon juice, salt and olive oil together. Toss arugula in 1/3ish of the dressing. Pour dressing over salad cubes. Salt to taste. Mound arugula in centre of salad bowl and serve.

So fresh you'll want to put a ring on it!

FENNEL ORANGE SALAD
4 loose handfuls arugula
1 large orange peeled and cut into wheels
1 fennel bulb shaved or sliced thin
3 thin slices red onion separated into rings
1/4 cup basil leaves torn roughly

VINAGRETTE
1/3 cup white balsamic vinegar
1 teaspoon Dijon mustard
Fresh cracked pepper
1/4 cup extra virgin olive oil
Himalayan pink sea salt

Layer salad ingredients in a large bowl. Dress with vinaigrette and season with a good salt to taste.

NOTES:

SANDWICH HEAVEN

Sandwiches are hearty, filling and convenient. Starchy goodness surrounds scrumptious fillings. I love a really good bread and don't want to waste my time on anything less! I grew up with homemade bread when Grandma came to visit - AMBROSIA otherwise supermarket fare. I thought for years that I didn't like sandwiches, but it was the commercial, pre-bagged bread. Experiment with different types and try the samples at the bakery. I believe fervently that any sandwich should be romanced by a pickle!

Throughout our lifetime we will make thousands of sandwiches for ourselves and our family. I adore taking help where I can find it, squeezable mayo and mustard, sliced cheese and pre-washed lettuce leaves. Never feel bad about gifting yourself the luxury of time. The important thing is that you're making yummy food instead of drive thru.

The sandwiches in here pack a variety of flavours, texture and temperatures. As always adjust to suit your own preference and taste, taste, taste.

Pillowy soft roll embraces sparky shards of pickled carrot, brash radish and slightly soapy (dirty girl) cilantro. All tethered by the earthy spice of that rascal Mr. Peanut!

BANH MI - BANH YU

2 carrots shredded
1/2 cups radish thinly sliced
1 small onion thinly sliced
1/2 jalapeño pepper minced or to taste
1 cup rice wine vinegar
1/2 cup water
1/4 cup sugar
1 cup peanut butter
3 tablespoon hoisin sauce
1 tablespoon soy sauce
4 soft sub buns
1/2 cup cilantro
16 basil leaves
1/2 English cucumber thinly sliced
1 cup Chinese (Napa) cabbage shredded
1/2 cup sriracha mayonnaise

Boil vinegar, sugar and water until sugar dissolves. Cool. Pour over carrots, radish, jalapeño and onion for 1/2 - 1 hour and drain.
Cream together peanut butter, soy sauce and sriracha. Smooth inside four buns. Top with pickled vegetables, cucumber, cabbage and herbs. Daub with sriracha mayonnaise.
This is a chock full, messy sandwich so I like to wrap it in parchment and cut diagonally.

Smokey grilled lettuce and crispy quesadilla stuffed with funky Brie. Add a luscious aioli to dunk - or bathe in!

QUESA-BRIE-A
Whole wheat tortillas
Dijon mustard
Brie
Spinach leaves roughly torn
Olive oil

Spread one side of tortilla with Dijon mustard and dot liberally with Brie cheese. Pile on the spinach and top with a second tortilla. Brown quesadilla on both sides in oil until cheese is ooey gooey. Douse with aioli.

AIOLI
½ cup mayonnaise
Three garlic cloves minced
One lemon juiced
¼ teaspoon Himalayan sea salt
Dash hot sauce

Stir all ingredients together. Taste and adjust seasonings accordingly.

Beat Box Lunch Rap - I like big wraps with some beans refried, avocado lovers can't deny, when the corn walks in with that chunky funky taste and leaves salsa on your face you say, yummm!!!

MEXICAN WRAP
1 cup assorted bell peppers sliced thin
½ cup red onion sliced thin
2 tablespoons olive oil
4 whole-wheat tortillas
1 cup refried beans
½ cup pepper jack cheese shredded
1 avocado sliced thin {squeeze lemon overtop to stay fresh}
½ cup corn kernels
Cilantro
1 cup salsa

Sauté onion and peppers in olive oil until tender. Spread one quarter cup bean dip on each tortilla. Sprinkle sparingly with cheese. Lovingly strew the avocado and corn over, top with the onion and pepper mix. Boldly blanket with chopped cilantro if you love it- or leave it off if you don't! Roll tightly and serve with salsa.

Egg salad sandwiches not only for the ladies auxiliary funerals. Creamy, crunchy and comforting with a horseradish requiem.

OPEN-FACED EGG SALAD SANDWICH
8 slices sour dough bread
Butter
Butter lettuce
8 hardboiled eggs peeled and diced
2 scallions minced
2 celery stalks minced
4 gherkins minced
1/3 cup parsley chopped
½ cup mayonnaise
¼ teaspoon wasabi
2 tablespoons Gherkin pickle juice
2 tablespoons melted butter

Himalayan sea salt and ground pepper to taste
Butter bread and pile on lettuce. Mash together rest of ingredients and mound onto bread. Serve with carrot sticks and radishes!

"Mommy? If there's a girl cheese sandwich, what's a boy cheese sandwich?"

GIRL CHEESE SANDWICH
8 slices fruit bread
Butter
Salt
Brie
½ cup chopped dried apricots
½ cup chopped pickled jalapeños
¼ cup Mayonnaise

Gently heat enough butter in skillet to cover bottom. Sprinkle with salt. Mix together apricots, jalapeños and mayonnaise. Spread relish on 4 slices of bread. Overlay bread with chunks of brie. Put top slice of bread on and butter outsides. Slowly toast to deep brown in skillet. Flip sandwiches, melt brie and brown other side. Let sit a minute before enjoying.

NOTES:

Vicky Gosse

SCRUMPTIOUS
STARTERS

SANDWICH HEAVEN

If I got to pick only one food to eat for the rest of my life, it would be dip. Appys always say party! I like to take mains and make them cute and small for hors d'oeuvres. They are usually portable, one handed bites (the other hand for your drink) that we chitchat and catch up over. An appy should be intensely flavourful, but leave you wanting more. I like to stick to a theme, a certain kind of food or a country. Of course, on birthdays the honouree gets their favourites.

Starters are the intro to dinner and set the tone for the entire meal. When starters are the meal or the only food, I try to go for variety of taste and texture, hot and cold.

My most humungous hint is....drum roll please...do as much as humanly possible before guests arrive. Enlist your congenial sister to help you chop and organize as your sous chef. When using one ingredient for several recipes, chop enough for all three at once and then portion out. Have a master list or you will be eating tofu stuffed mushroom caps for breakfast the next day. Cheers!!!

Hummuses or hummussi? Our favourite creamy chickpea dip - sassified! Earthy beet, sweet carrot, and spring green herb hummus. They're all humdingers!!!

BASIC HUMMUS
1 - 15 ounce tin chickpeas
2 cloves garlic
1 lemon (juiced)
½ teaspoon cumin
¼ cup tahini
¼ cup(ish) water
2 tablespoon Olive Oil
½ teaspoon Himalayan pink sea salt

Blitz all together in food processor to desired consistency, adding more or less water as needed.

BEET HUMMUS
½ cup basic hummus
4 small beets (boiled or roasted)
2 inch chunk ginger (cut into coins)
Olive oil or water

Whiz into a luscious smooth paste, adding extra olive oil or water if necessary.

CARROT HUMMUS
½ cup basic hummus
8 large carrots (roasted-bit of char is good)
¼ cup maple syrup
½ teaspoon cumin
½ teaspoon cayenne pepper
Olive oil or water

Buzz carrots into hummus with syrup and cumin. Leave a little chunkier for texture.

HERBED HUMMUS
1 cup basic hummus
¾ cup packed fresh herbs (basil, parsley, dill, cilantro, thyme)
½ lemon (juiced)
Olive oil or water

Whirl everything into a fluffy green concoction. Rosemary, sage and chives can also be used but are more assertive. I always smell my herb mixture and adjust accordingly.

Angelic devilled eggs. Velvety and lush with a spirited buzz. Thanks Mum!!

DEVILLED EGGS
12 hard-boiled eggs (halved)
1/3 cup mayonnaise
1/2 teaspoon Himalayan pink sea salt
1 tablespoon gherkin pickle juice
3 drops Tabasco
1 tablespoon Dijon mustard
2 tablespoon celery finely minced
*paprika and chive flowers for garnish (optional but pretty)

In a small bowl mash together egg yolks with all other ingredients. Spoon or pipe back into white shells. Sprinkle with paprika and garnish with chive flowers. Refrigerate for 20 minutes before serving.

A warm, gentle, vegan start to a meal that is familiar and comforting, but with enough of an edge to interest and excite!! What more can you ask of lowly vegetables. Feel free to use any of the below as a tasty side dish!

VEGAN VEGGIE PLATTER (oxymoron?)

BRUSSEL SPROUTS
2 cups brussels sprouts halved
3 tablespoons each olive oil & balsamic vinegar (I like coffee flavoured)
Himalayan pink sea salt and fresh ground pepper

Roast until brown and tender.

CRISPY BROCCOLI
4 cups broccoli florets
3 tablespoons each olive oil & Lemon juice
1/2 teaspoon each onion powder, garlic powder

Mix oil, lemon and spices together and massage broccoli. Roast until edges are crispy.

ROASTED CARROTS
12 carrots sliced lengthwise
1/4 cup olive oil
1/2 teaspoon each cumin, salt & pepper
1 orange pulverized
2 inch chunk ginger grated

Smear carrots with oil and spices. Roast until browned and caramelized. Stir together orange pulp with grated ginger and pile on carrots.

SUGAR SNAP PEAS
2 cups sugar snap peas
1 tablespoon garlic olive oil
1 tablespoon lime juice
Pink Himalayan sea salt
Fresh ground pepper

Anoint peas with oil, lime, salt and pepper and grill until
lightly charred and softened.

SWEET BELL PEPPERS
1 each red, yellow and orange pepper - cut into strips
2 tablespoons olive oil
2 tablespoons water
1/2 teaspoon Italian seasoning
Himalayan pink sea salt and fresh cracked pepper to taste

Mix and roast until peppers brown on edges.

BABY EGGPLANT
6 baby eggplants sliced in half
2 tablespoons olive oil
1/2 teaspoon dried oregano
1/2 lemon juiced
2 cloves of garlic minced

Jumble en masse, roast until soft. Do not put oil on
eggplant prior to roasting. They are like little sponges and
will suck it up and become oily!

YELLOW SQUASH
6 yellow squash - quartered lengthwise
2 tablespoons olive oil
2 tablespoons lemon juice
1/2 teaspoon Greek seasoning

Christen squash with juice, oil and seasoning. Roast until al dente and fragrant.

ROASTED GREEN ONION
1 bunch green onion

Drizzle with olive oil. Lightly char on your grill or under a broiler.

ROASTED GARLIC
Cut the top off bulb of garlic. Drizzle with olive oil and a sprinkling of water. Wrap loosely in parchment paper then in tinfoil. Roast in oven 40 to 60 minutes. Unwrap, squeeze out garlic and enjoy!! This takes away the harsh burn of garlic and it becomes sweet and buttery.

TAHINI DIP
1/3 cup tahini
2 tablespoons lemon juice
2 tablespoons water
1/2 teaspoon cumin
Himalayan sea salt and black pepper to taste
Cream all together. Thin with water to the desired consistency.

Arrange all the vegetables on a large cutting board or platter in an aesthetically pleasing manner with the dip. I like to serve the dip in a footed glass (like a wine or margherita glass), so that it's easily accessible.

She reclines in a purple pout, glistening with unctuous opulence. Your tongue tingles with the first lick of rosemary and a garlicky taunt. Nip the tender flesh and gently tease out the pit. She explodes into a fiery flood of briny umami. Yes! Yes!! Yes!!! I'll have what she's having.

ORGASMIC OLIVES
3 cups Kalamata olives
5 garlic cloves halved
5 sprigs fresh rosemary lightly bruised
3-5 red chilies halved lengthwise
2 glugs olive oil

Pour everything into a Ziploc baggie and massage. Marinate a few hours. Tip into serving dish and enjoy with drinks.
Olives are also delicious as a topping for pasta or stirred into eggs. I like them on pizza or chopped in a sandwich.

Crisply clean with a candy-like crunch: A cruciferous crop of crudité carpaccio. (If Picasso and Julia Child had a love baby)

CARPACCIO OF VEGETABLE
2 beets sliced paper-thin (mandolin)
2 carrots sliced thin (mandolin or veg peeler)
2 large florets of cauliflower sliced paper-thin (stem and floret intact - like a tree)
8 razor thin slices of jalapeño

DRESSING
2 tablespoons of olive oil
One lemon juiced
2 tablespoons ginger marmalade
2 tablespoons capers
Combine all ingredients together. Marinate vegetables in dressing for at least half an hour, separately so colours don't diffuse.

SAUTEED BEET GREENS
4 cups beet greens and stems chopped
2 tablespoons olive oil
Fresh ground pepper and Himalayan pink sea salt to taste
Heat oil in skillet. Rinse greens and stems, rough chop, and add to skillet without drying. Lightly sauté with salt and pepper.

To assemble - divide sautéed greens onto four plates. Arrange vegetables prettily. Pour leftover marinade (except beet) over all.

The much maligned, yet nutritional darling, quinoa, is delectable when partying with risqué red chilies, voluptuous mango and crisply sweet watermelon.

QUINOA WATERMELON WEDGE

2 cups cooked quinoa (add bouillon or miso to cooking water for a flavour boost)
1 cup red lentils cooked
3 spring onions chopped fine
1 red Thai chili minced
1/2 English cucumber seeded and diced small (1/4 inch)
1/2 cup tomato seeded and diced (1/4 inch)
1/2 red pepper diced small(1/4 inch)
1/2 cup mango diced small
1/2 cup parsley and cilantro chopped fine
3 tablespoon fresh lime juice
Zest of lime
3 tablespoons rice wine vinegar
1/3 cup extra virgin olive oil
Fresh cracked black pepper and Himalayan pink sea salt to taste

Mix all together and break up lumps with a fork. Taste and add salt and pepper as needed.

Icy cold watermelon
Cut watermelon into 2" wedges. Mound a quenelle (football shape) of quinoa onto each wedge.

You can turn this into a great salad by cubing the watermelon and mixing it into the quinoa. Eat it quickly as the watermelon doesn't keep!

The opulent, velvet creaminess of avocado is livened up with a sparky sting of lime then spanked by jalapeno.

GUACAMOLE
2 large avocados perfectly ripe (slight give when pressed)
1/2 teaspoon Himalayan pink sea salt
1 tablespoon fresh lime juice
1 spring onion sliced very thin
1 jalapeno pepper minced
2 tablespoons fresh cilantro chopped fine
2-3 grinds fresh cracked pepper
1/2 tomato seeded and chopped small

Mash avocados to desired texture. Add in salt and lime juice. Gently stir in all the other ingredients. Let sit for an hour so flavours can meld. Serve with nacho chips, on chili, or in a taco!

Creamy and starchy with a salty spark from briny olive shards. Fiber is the new protein! (winky face)

REFRIED BEAN DIP
2 tins vegetarian refried beans
2 tins mild green chilies
1/2 cup each green and black olives chopped
1 bunch green onion (chopped 1/4 inch)
2 cups cheese (jack, mozzarella, cheddar or vegan) grated
1 cup fresh cilantro chopped fine

Stir together beans, chilies, olives and onion. Spread out into rectangular cake pan. Blanket with shredded cheese and bake until hot, bubbly and brown. Christen your offering with cilantro. So good with nacho chips, on a taco or blobbed onto a green salad as a dressing. This recipe is easily doubled or halved, depending on how popular you are!

Salty, sweet, crunchy and sour, blanketed in cheesy goodness! A fresh take on a classic. With a nod to Nourish Vegetarian Bistro in Banff!

NOD TO NOURISH NACHOS
1 bag whole grain nacho
2-3 finely chopped tablespoons each of the following:

green onion	mushrooms
green beans	kidney beans
Brussel sprouts	lima beans
cilantro	navy beans
green olives	black-eyed beans
Kalamata olives	pumpkin seeds
strawberries	sweet peppers
jalapeño pepper	diced radish
mild green chilies	garbanzo beans
carrot	kale
white kidney beans	yellow beets
raisins	green apple
gherkins	poppy seeds
dark chocolate chips	Napa cabbage

or anything else that sounds good to you.
Beans, fruits, veggies, nuts and seeds are all awesome toppers!
2 cups of shredded jack cheese
2 cups of shredded mozzarella (or meltable vegan mozzarella cheese)

Line 2 large cookie sheets with parchment paper. Evenly distribute your favourite nachos over each sheet. Sprinkle with small amount of cheeses. Sparingly strew all your ingredients over nachos. Blanket nachos with shredded mozzarella, jack or vegan cheese.
Bake 15-20 minutes at 375 until cheese is ooey gooey and melted. Enjoy with salsa, sour cream, lime wedges and guacamole. Ole!!

Sneaky little lentils! So virtuous and innocent. Until you anoint them with provocative spices and delectable dried fruit.

LOVING THE LENTIL DIP
1 tin lentils drained and rinsed
1/3 each red, yellow, and orange pepper diced fine
4 green onions sliced thin
1/2 cup dried cranberries (any dried fruit) chopped

DRESSING
1/3 cup EVOO
1/4 c apple cider vinegar
2 teaspoons Dijon mustard
1 teaspoon curry powder
1/2 tsp cinnamon
1/8 tsp cloves
1/2 lemon juiced

Mix together lentils, veggies and dried fruit. In a measuring cup whisk dressing ingredients en masse and pour over lentils. Let sit at least 2 hours or overnight. This is scrumptious as a dip with poppadum's or tortilla chips. Trust me, this dip is surprisingly addictive!

There's something so sensuous about eating with your fingers. Little bites of salty crunch, grassy herb, fresh bursts of sweet, and pungent, oily goodness. An overload of sensations. □

VEGAN ANTIPASTI PLATTER
Beets spiralized or shaved thin and spritzed with orange
Tabbouleh (from deli)
Green Olive Tapenade (recipe below)
Cherry tomatoes with fresh basil
Pickled artichoke hearts
Black grapes
Brown rice and/or lentils (cooked)
Jicama with lime juice and cayenne
Crusty freshly baked bread (black olive)
Extra virgin olive oil
Good quality balsamic vinegar

Arrange on a platter. Swirl bread thru oil and vinegar, mix and match dips and spreads, and enjoy!

GREEN OLIVE TAPENADE
1 cup green olives (pitted and drained)
1/2 cup giardiniera vegetables drained
2 tablespoons capers
2 cloves garlic minced
Pinch of dried chilies
1/2 lemon juiced (2 tablespoons)
1/4 cup extra virgin olive oil

Pulse together in a food processor. Refrigerate and shape into a quenelle
(football) with two spoons to plate. Also yummy with crackers or on pasta.

Creamy dairy goodness with a garlic hum.
TZATZIKI
1 cup Greek Yogurt
1 mini cucumber (grated and squeezed dry-ish)
3 tablespoon minced garlic
¼ cup dill (minced)
½ teaspoon Himalayan sea salt

Mix gently. Serve with lightly toasted pita.

NOTES:

Vicky Gosse

SUPPER

In a perfect world my happy family leisurely gathers around the dining room table for a gastronomic feast. But that could just be my family! Haha, in truth this happens rarely. Dinners are often rushed, little time for cooking and everyone on a different schedule. In addition, there's gluten free, allergies, lactose intolerant, meatatarians and one who doesn't like cucumbers. Dinners need to be flexible, fuss-free and easily adjustable.

My least favourite question of the day is, "What's for supper?" I used to decide on beef, chicken, pork or fish? Now I start with the vegetable. What's in the fridge, the garden or amazing at the supermarket? I shop with my recipe book in hand as a reference. Vegetables are the star and if there's a meat eater you can always throw in a hunk of chicken or fish, a steak or a pork chop, and sauce it the same. Anything meat can do, tofu can do better!

Beautifully bland squash sublimely infused with crunchy cabbage, salty sweet soy and the seductive heat of ginger.

SPAGHETTI SQUASH CHOW MEIN
2 small spaghetti squash halved lengthwise remove seeds
2 tablespoons of olive oil
1 bunch spring onion sliced diagonally
3 cloves garlic minced
2 inch chunk of ginger minced
1 bag coleslaw cabbage with carrots
¼ cup vegetable broth
¼ cup soy sauce
¼ cup ketchup
½ teaspoon dried ginger
½ teaspoon garlic powder
½ teaspoon ground pepper
Cilantro to garnish

Bake squash in 350 degree oven for 30 minutes or until tender. Scrape strands out with fork and set aside. Heat oil in large skillet and gently sauté onions for 2 minutes. Add garlic, ginger, coleslaw, and broth. Strew squash over and drizzle with soy, ketchup and spice mixture. Lovingly toss to combine and serve with brown rice if you want to make it more complicated!

Smoky cauliflower all sweet and sticky with folksy sautéed veg stung by the tart spank of the lemon.

BARBECUED CAULIFLOWER STEAK
One head cauliflower
2 tablespoons olive oil
Himalayan pink sea salt and fresh cracked black pepper to taste
2 tablespoons barbecue sauce

Carefully cut cauliflower lengthwise into four steaks using the stem to keep each one together. Drizzle with olive oil and sprinkle with salt and pepper. Grill on barbecue for five minutes, turn, grill an additional five minutes. Brush with barbecue sauce.

Virtuous veggie pasta falls into the slutty salinity of "ladies of the evening" sauce.

ZUGHETTI PUTTANESCA

Break out the spiralizer and crank out enough for four. Or - halve your zucchini's and scrape out seeds. Slice into ribbons with vegetable peeler or mandolin. (4 medium squash)

PUTTANESCA SAUCE
1/4 cup olive oil
5 cloves garlic minced or crushed
1 bunch green onion chopped
1 teaspoon soy sauce
1/2 teaspoon pepper
3/4 teaspoon dried chili flakes
1/4 cup capers
1 cup Kalamata olives pitted
 28 oz. tin diced tomatoes
1 teaspoon each dried oregano, basil
1/2 cup fresh basil rough chopped

Heat oil in a sauté pan. Cook garlic, onion, soy sauce, pepper and dried chili flakes over medium heat for two minutes. Add rest of ingredients and simmer 10 minutes. Toss in zughetti* and heat thru, strew with fresh basil.

Exotic earthy eastern flavours are seduced by spunky spinach - so sexy!

CURRIED CHICKPEAS WITH SPINACH
2 tablespoons olive oil
1 small onion diced
3 cloves garlic minced
3 tablespoons curry
¼ teaspoon cinnamon
¼ teaspoon cayenne pepper
¼ teaspoon cumin
¼ teaspoon ginger
2 tins chickpeas/garbanzo beans drained
2 cups tomato sauce
4 cups spinach chopped
Cilantro to garnish
Plain Greek yogurt

Heat oil in large skillet with onion. Sauté until soft and add garlic and spices. Bung in tomato sauce and beans and heat through. Gently fold in spinach and garnish with fresh cilantro. Dollop with plain Greek yogurt if you like a creamy texture.

Terribly hearty rice made vibrant with veggies and the ubiquitous egg.

VEGGIE FRIED RICE
3 tablespoons EVOO
½ cup onion
½ cup mushrooms finely diced
2 inch chunk ginger micro-planed
¼ cup broccoli bite sized
¼ cup carrot finely diced
¼ cup celery finely diced
¼ cup bell pepper finely diced
1 splash of soy sauce
1 splash of rice wine vinegar
1 tablespoon butter
6 whole eggs
Himalayan sea salt and fresh ground pepper to taste
4 cups cooked brown rice
½ cup cilantro chopped-optional

Sauté onion in one tablespoon olive oil until softened. Toss in ginger, soy sauce and vinegar. Add rest of vegetables and cook until tender crisp. Set aside on a plate. Using the same skillet, on a low heat, melt butter and stir eggs until barely set. Season and add to plate of veggies. Heat 2 tablespoons of olive oil to medium-high and spread rice over bottom of pan. Cook until crust forms. Flip rice over and crisp up the other side. Gently toss rice, vegetables and egg to distribute. Garnish with cilantro.
Fiery chili romances Garlicky Bok Choy on the side.

Divinely bland eggplant picks up the vegetabley goodness of onion, garlic and peppers. Zucchini bathes in saucy tomato and lemon, with bread to unify.

RATATAT IT TO ME RATATOUILLE
3 cups eggplant diced
3 cups zucchini diced
One large onion diced
2 cloves of garlic minced
1 each of orange, red, yellow and green pepper diced
6 Roma tomatoes quartered
3 tablespoons olive oil
Himalayan sea salt and fresh ground pepper
3 tablespoons fresh tarragon
½ cup basil cut into ribbons
½ cup seasoned bread crumbs
2 lemons zested and juiced

Anoint veggies with olive oil, season with salt, pepper and garlic. Spread out on cookie sheet and roast until tender. Tip into baking dish and toss with fresh herbs and lemon juice. Top with bread crumbs and lemon zest. Broil until golden brown and crunchy. Serve with rice or a chunk of crusty bread.

Succulent fibers of chik'n* drenched in lashings of spicy-smoky barbeque sauce. Enrobed in ooey gooey cheese. Spiked with fresh cilantro greenness and all on the pizza!

BARBECUE CHICK'N PIZZA
2 thin whole wheat pizza crust or gluten free
1 cup barbecue sauce
3 Chik'n* breasts shredded sliced fine
½ red onion sliced thin
2 cups pizza cheese shredded
½ cup cilantro chopped
Extra barbeque sauce to drizzle

Coat chick'n in half a cup of barbeque sauce. Spread 1/4 cup of barbeque sauce over each pizza crust using the back of a spoon or ladle to even out. Distribute chik'n* over each pie. Mound cheese over all. Bake on pizza stone or cookie sheet. When brown and bubbly scatter with cilantro and trickle with barbeque sauce.

*Chik'n is a vegetarian alternative to chicken.

Donut. Burger. Need I say more? Drop the mic.

DONUT BURGER
8 yeast donuts crullers or honey glaze
4 veggie patties
Red leaf or butter lettuce
Pickled onion
Wasabi mayo

Barbeque your favourite veggie patties. Assemble burger with donut, lettuce, burger, wasabi mayo, large pile of pickled onion and second donut. Spear with a skewer or eat!

PICKLED ONION
1 red onion sliced thinly
1 cup white vinegar
3 tablespoons salt
Dissolve salt in warm vinegar and pour over onion. Let sit 1-12 hours. Drain.

WASABI MAYO
1/2 cup mayonnaise not miracle whip
1 teaspoon wasabi powder
1 teaspoon water
2 tablespoons lemon juice

Mix wasabi and water into paste. Stir into mayonnaise and thin with lemon juice.

DONUT SLIDERS
These are an awesome appetizer using the 50 pack of Timbits and cutting each patty into six. Use a pick through each slider and nestle closely together on serving tray as they are a bit wobbly.

Funky brussels sprouts, sweet chewy apricots,
garlicky pistou and tangy thrashings of musty
balsamic glaze.

BRUSSEL SPROUT PIZZA
Two whole wheat pizza shells or gluten free
1/2 cup pistou* or pesto
1/2 cup roasted brussels sprouts cut into coins
12 dried apricots sliced thin
Balsamic glaze to drizzle

Divide pistou over each pizza shell and spread to outer
edge. Top with roasted brussel sprouts and dried apricots.
Sprinkle with Himalayan pink sea salt. Bake until warm
and fragrant. Concentric circles of balsamic complete this
vegan gastronomic masterpiece.

*PISTOU (basil oil)
1 cup basil leaves
1/2 cup extra Virgin olive oil
3 cloves garlic
1/2 teaspoon Himalayan pink sea salt
Blitz until smooth(ish)

Sooty fumes evoke porky goodness on a sweetly barbecued tofu "ham steak".

BARBECUE TOFU STEAK
2 bricks pressed tofu
1/2 cup hickory barbecue sauce
1/2 teaspoon liquid smoke
2 tablespoons olive oil

Slice each brick in half horizontally and then half again, making four steak per brick. Marinate in sauce, smoke and oil for thirty minutes and grill each side.

Serve with Greek Roasted Zucchini and Corn on the Cob. Virginal zucchini is spritzed with lime and sassed with Greek spices. Grilled corn only needs a salty sprinkle.

The silky blandness of tofu is magic when marinated in dulcet maple syrup and zippy garlic sriracha. Pair with nutty brown rice and crunchy green broccoli.

SRIRACHA TOFU
2 bricks firm tofu cubed
1/3 cup maple syrup
1/3 cup sriracha
1 tablespoon olive oil

Cut each brick of tofu in half lengthwise then cube. Marinate for at least thirty minutes. Bake in 375° oven for 20 minutes.

BROWN RICE
Cook enough brown rice for four as directed on package. I like to use vegetable broth or miso paste in the water for extra flavour.

Serve with the side Garlic Sautéed Broccoli

Sweet and spicy, smoky citrus tofu is grilled Korean style.

KOREAN BARBEQUED TOFU SKEWERS
2 bricks extra firm tofu
2 tablespoons brown sugar
1 tablespoon olive oil
1 tablespoon soy sauce
1 teaspoon gochujang
1 lime zested and juiced
1 clove garlic minced
Salt and pepper to taste

Cube each tofu brick. Bake at 350° degrees for 10 minutes. Marinate in rest of ingredients. Skewer tofu cubes and grill. Baste with marinade.

Finger licking good with Salt Crusted Baby Potatoes and Steamed Green Beans.

Savoury and scrumptious savoy cabbage is tenderly caramelized and sauced over linguine.

CABBAGE LINGUINE
1 box linguine noodles
1/3 cup extra virgin olive oil
1/2 teaspoon dried chili flakes
1 medium head savoy cabbage shredded
1 onion sliced fine
1/3 cup celery sliced fine
1/3 cup chopped parsley
1 teaspoon tamari or soy sauce
Fresh cracked pepper lots
3 Tablespoons chives
4 hardboiled eggs if desired

Cook noodles in heavily salted water and drain.
In a skillet slowly caramelize cabbage, onion, celery and chill flakes in olive oil. In 20 minutes (or when browned) add in parsley, tamari and drained noodles. Mix together and garnish with pepper, chives and chopped hardboiled egg.

Assertively flavourful, sautéed onion and garlic celebrate bell pepper. Sweet tomato is enveloped in ricey goodness and mild chili heat.

SPANISH RICE STUFFED PEPPERS
4 bell peppers tops cut off and seeds removed
3 tablespoons olive oil
1 medium onion diced small
Fresh ground black pepper and Himalayan pink sea salt to taste
1 1/2 cups uncooked white rice
4 bell pepper tops diced small
2 cloves garlic minced
1 tin mild green chilis
2 cups vegetable broth (reserve 4 tablespoons)
1 cup chunky salsa

Heat oil in a large skillet over medium. Stir in onion and cook 5 minutes. Mix in rice, peppers, salt and pepper, stirring often. When rice is golden stir in garlic for 30 seconds, and add all the rest of the ingredients. Cover and simmer over a low heat for 15 minutes until liquid is absorbed. The rice should be a little al dente. Spoon rice mixture into 4 bell peppers and sprinkle with reserved broth. Nestle together into baking dish with 1/3 cup water and cover with lid or foil. Bake at 375 degrees for 10 minutes to steam peppers. A dusting of salt, pepper and cilantro tops your masterpiece. My husband loves a big hunk of cheese broiled over top.

As delicious to eat as it is fun to say! Crunchy rice, pickled veg, savoury greens, crispy tofu and gochujang!

BIBIMBAP
4 cups cooked rice
1 medium carrot cut into matchsticks
1 medium bell pepper cut into matchsticks
1/2 small red onion sliced thin
1 cup white vinegar
1/2 cup water
1/4 cup sugar
2 cups shredded Chinese (Napa) cabbage
2 cups shredded spinach
1/2 cup green beans sliced thinly
2 tablespoons extra virgin olive oil
1 teaspoon sesame oil
1/2 English cucumber sliced thin
2 radishes diced small
4 tablespoons gochujang
1 tablespoon soy sauce

Cook rice according to package directions. (This is a great recipe to use up left over rice.) While rice is cooking heat vinegar, water and sugar until dissolved. Pour over the bell pepper, carrots and onion in separate bowls. Cover and let stand to pickle. In a heavy bottomed skillet heat oils and sauté separately cabbage, spinach and green beans. To make sauce, mix gochujang, soy sauce, 1 tablespoon pickling liquid and 1 tablespoon water. When rice is done, crisp it up in the skillet. Divide the rice into four large bowls. Divide all the vegetables over top. Drizzle with gochujang sauce. I use 1 teaspoon on mine but my family likes it spicy and uses a lot more.   Enjoy!

Yeah, yeah, yeah. I know! Everyone does vegetarian chili and they're all special. But this one is... good! It's all in the accoutrements! Guacamole, coleslaw, corn chips, spring onion, cilantro and for non-vegans con queso, sour cream and pepper jack cheese.

CROCKPOT VEGAN CHILI
In a large crockpot dump in;
1 large onion diced
4 cloves garlic chopped
2 peppers chopped
2 large carrots chopped
1 cup mushrooms chopped
3 ribs celery diced fine
1 jalapeño minced (more or less to taste)
2 - 28 oz. tins tomatoes
2 - 15 oz. tins kidney beans drained
1 - 15 oz. each tin garbanzo beans, black beans and corn kernels (drained)
2 tins green chilis
1 cup tomato sauce
1 beer
3 tablespoons chili powder
2 tablespoons dried oregano
1 tablespoon cumin
2 tablespoons onion powder
1 tablespoon cocoa powder
1 teaspoon each salt and pepper or to taste

I love to eat this in a large bowl with coleslaw on one side, guac on top, a sprinkle of onion and corn chips.
Sometimes I do dairy and I like habanero jack cheese shreds melting right on top of the hot chili.

Creamy curry spiked with lemon and a hint of heat.
Beautiful with broccoli on a bed of basmati □.

CURRIED BROCCOLI
4 cups Broccoli florets
2 tablespoons EVOO
1/2 cup diced onion
1 clove minced garlic
1 tablespoon curry powder
1/2 teaspoon ginger
1/2 teaspoon dried chili pepper
1 tin coconut milk
lemon wedges

Heat olive oil in a large skillet and sauté onions. Add the
garlic and spices stirring continuously until warm and
fragrant. Toss broccoli in with the aromatics and pour in
the coconut milk. Simmer to thicken and broccoli is tender
crisp. Serve over basmati rice with a squeeze of lemon.

Exotically earthy, fiendishly fiery, and vibrant with vinegar! This curry seduces with its promise of danger.

VINDALOO LENTILS
1 tablespoon olive oil
2 cups onion rough chopped
3 cloves minced garlic
1/2 teaspoon each cayenne, turmeric, cinnamon
1 tablespoon each curry powder, cumin
1 cup water
1 28 ounce tin diced tomatoes
2 bell peppers diced
1 tablespoon ginger grated
1 chili, minced
1/3 cup kombucha vinegar (or apple cider)
2 cups vegetable broth
1 1/2 cup dried lentils
Yogurt and cilantro to garnish

Heat oil in a Dutch oven and sauté onions to soften. Add spices and toast until fragrant. Simmer in 1 cup of water for 5 minutes. Stir in tomatoes, peppers, ginger and half the chilis. Save the other half for those who want it extra spicy. Pour in the vinegar and broth and let simmer 10 minutes. Sprinkle in the lentils and cook15 minutes until tender. Serve warm over basmati rice or naan bread. Garnish with yogurt and cilantro!

Butter(less) Chicken(less)
A sweet and mild, creamy, tomato curry. It is luscious and voluptuous, and a truly decadent gastronomic experience.

VEGAN BUTTER CHICKEN
2 large onions chopped
1/4 cup olive oil
3 cloves minced garlic
2 tablespoons garam masala
2 teaspoons curry powder
1 teaspoon chili powder
2 teaspoons ground cumin
1/2 teaspoon ground ginger
Himalayan pink sea salt and ground pepper to taste
1 28 ounce tin tomato puree
2 tins coconut milk
2 tins garbanzo beans, rinsed and drained
1 large sweet potato cut into large chunks
Pea sprouts or cilantro to garnish

Sauté onions in olive oil until caramelized. Add all the spices and stir until fragrant. Pour in the beans, tomatoes and coconut milk. Gently stir in the sweet potatoes, and cook until tender. I like to use the crockpot so I can forget about it until dinner. If it seems too runny you can thicken with cornstarch and water, or if it's too thick add a little more liquid.
I like it saucy and served over rice. Garnish and enjoy.

A classic. Fresh tangy tomato sauce, creamy buffalo mozzarella, fragrant basil. Ciao Bella □

MARGHERITA PIZZA
2 whole wheat pizza shells (or gluten free)
Extra virgin olive oil
Favourite tomato sauce
1 large fresh buffalo mozzarella ball packed in water
2 - 3 Roma tomatoes sliced 1/4 inch thick
1/2 cup of basil leaves

Brush pizza shells with olive oil and salt from a height. Ladle scant amount of tomato sauce over each and spread to cover. Roughly tear mozzarella into chunks and distribute evenly, ensuring each slice has cheese. Ditto tomato slices. Tuck basil leaves over and under cheese and tomatoes. Cook on pizza stone or baking sheet lined with parchment until cheese has melted and edges are browned and crisp. Let sit a few minutes. Slice and savour!

Mamma Mia! Here we go again. My, my! Another tofu recipe!

GREEK MARINATED TOFU
2 bricks pressed tofu cut into eighths
2 tablespoons olive oil
1/2 a lemon juiced
2 cloves garlic minced
2 tablespoons dried oregano
1 teaspoon dried mint
1/2 teaspoon fresh cracked pepper

Dry tofu and place in a large freezer bag. Dump in all the rest of the ingredients and marinate for an hour. Preheat oven to 450 degrees and cook tofu 15-20 minutes until heated through and starting to brown and crisp on the edges.

Ok. This is NOT spaghetti, but it is divinely bland and redolent of every flavour it bathes in.

MEXICAN SPAGHETTI SQUASH
1/2 spaghetti squash per person
1/3 cup favorite salsa
1 tablespoon chopped green or red onion
1/4 cup each black beans, corn, diced tomato
Minced jalapeño to taste
Pepper jack or vegan melting cheese
Cilantro to taste
1/4 avocado diced
1/4 lime juiced
Sour cream or almond cream to top

Cut squash in half lengthwise and scrape out seeds with a spoon. Roast in oven at 375 degrees for 30 - 45 mins until tender and lightly charred. Using a towel pull out squash and scuff with a fork to separate into strands. Toss with salsa and veg. Top with "cheese" and broil until bubbly. Garnish with avocado, cilantro, a squeeze of lime and Himalayan pink sea salt to taste. Almond cream or sour cream modifies the heat level if needed. You may get to add extra filling if your squash is large!

Poke is a fresh, flavourful Hawaiian raw fish salad (similar to ceviche) but can be made vegan with tofu. The ponzu sauce is bracingly acidic with a throaty salinity evocative of soy. Crisp raw veggies add crunch and brown rice is cozily nutty.

PRETTY POKE
2 cups cooked brown rice
1 brick tofu extra firm or pressed
2 scallions sliced thinly at a diagonal
1 teaspoon toasted sesame seeds
1 tablespoon Braggs Liquid Soy
1 tablespoon toasted sesame oil
1-2 tablespoon seaweed finely sliced
Additional Toppings
avocado sliced and spritzed with lime
carrot sliced thin with veg peeler or mandolin
small cucumber sliced very thin
1/4 cup pineapple diced small
cherry tomatoes sliced
2 tablespoons lentils
3 tablespoons vegan kimchi

PONZU SAUCE
3 teaspoons rice wine vinegar
⅛ cup mirin
⅛ cup Braggs Liquid Soy
⅛ cup fresh squeezed orange juice (half an orange)
1 tablespoon fresh lime juice

Blot the tofu well with kitchen towel. Dice into quarter inch cubes and season with salt and pepper. Marinate in scallions, sesame seeds, Braggs, sesame oil, and seaweed. Quickly stir-fry to meld flavours and crisp the scallions. Tofu can drink in the liquid so you may need to add more oil and Braggs in equal portions. Make your quick Ponzu sauce by whisking ingredients together. Divide the rice in two large bowls. Pile poke salad high in the centre, and surround with additional toppings. Spoon the fresh ponzu sauce over the veggies and sprinkle with sesame seeds. Serve with chop sticks and sriracha.

*Braggs liquid Soy is a gluten free alternative to soy sauce
*radishes, edamame, beets, cabbage, pickled ginger, almond, cashews, pomegranate and mango are all excellent toppings

This Greek dish runs the gamut from tangy with citrus accents to savoury with strong bold feta.

GREEK SPAGHETTI SQUASH
1 spaghetti squash halved lengthwise and seeds removed
Handful of Kalamata olives seeded and slivered
Handful of grape tomatoes slivered
Feta cheese roughly chopped (vegan available)
1/3 cup green or red onion finely diced
Large handful of fresh dill or basil, finely chopped
Extra virgin olive oil
1 lemon juiced
Himalayan pink sea salt and fresh cracked black pepper

Cut the spaghetti squash in half lengthwise, and use a spoon to scrape out the seeds. Brush lightly with olive oil and salt and pepper. Bake the spaghetti squash face down approximately 40 minutes at 375 degrees. Remove from oven and scuff with a fork to separate into strands. Top the squash with veg and cheese. Make a quick vinaigrette by combining lemon juice, fresh herbs, salt, pepper and whisk in the grassy EVOO. Pour over all and serve in squash shell. The amount of toppings depends on the amount of squash. Size does matter!!!

Earthy, elegant, and pink!

BEETAGHETTI
4 medium beets spiralized
3 tablespoons extra virgin olive oil
2 cloves garlic minced
1/4 teaspoon red chili flakes
1 cup sour cream or almond cream
1/4 cup fresh dill chopped
1/4 cup fresh basil chopped
Himalayan pink sea salt and fresh ground pepper

Boil beets in salted water for 3 to 5 minutes until tender crisp. Heat olive oil in skillet and gently sauté garlic and red chili. Meekly toss in spiralized beets and delicately stir in almond or sour cream, dill and basil. Season with salt and pepper.

NOTES:

SUCCULENT
SIDES

Vicky Gosse

SIDES

I frigging love sides!!! They're so creative, the jewelry of the meal. Gone are the days of grey flaccid 'once upon a time' green beans. We are heralding inventive cooking methods, light but flavour packed dressings and roasting anything that doesn't move.

Roasting veggies brings out their inherent sweetness, especially on root vegetables. The caramelization pleases the palette of even picky eaters, and most vegetables can be prepped way ahead of time and then just thrown in the oven. Roasting is one of the most healthful ways of cooking because it's not diluted and nothing is left behind. The leftovers can be re-heated, used on a sandwich, in soups, on pasta or in an omelet.

That universally loathed little fart bomb Brussel sprout is POOF! magically transformed by cutting in half and roasted with a drizzle of balsamic. Scary artichokes are wrestled into a tasty topic of conversation and the mundanely phallic carrot transitions into an orgasmic, come hither drag queen. Let your freak flag fly!

GREEK ROASTED ZUCCHINI
4 medium zucchinis cut into thick coins
1 tablespoon olive oil
1/2 lemon juiced and zested
1 teaspoon greek spices
Himalayan sea salt and ground pepper

Toss everything together on a cookie sheet and roast until tender.

CORN ON THE COB
Shuck corn and grill on the barbecue until hot, charred and tender.

FLAVOUR BOMBS
Sprinkle with sea salt if desired.
For Mexican street corn, sprinkle with cojita cheese.
Simply serve corn alongside lime wedges and cayenne pepper.

ZESTY BUTTER
Mix up a compound butter by softening butter and stirring in lime zest, cumin and honey. Wrap in cling film and shape into a log. Twirl the ends to seal and pop into the fridge. When chilled, cut into coins and offer up beside the corn.

Moist and sweet with a crumbly texture and a lingering warmth. Smear spicy honey butter with abandon and serve with a chaste salad.

SPICY CORNBREAD
1 1/2 cup cornmeal
1/2 cup flour
1 1/2 teaspoon baking powder
1 teaspoon Himalayan sea salt
1 1/4 cup buttermilk
1 egg
1 tablespoon honey
1/2 cup corn
1/2 tin mild green chilies

Preheat oven to 375 degrees. Combine all the dry ingredients. Whisk the egg into the buttermilk and honey. Gently stir into the dry ingredients until just combined. Add the corn and peppers. Pour into greased 8" baking dish. Bake 30 minutes until top is slightly browned and a toothpick inserted into the middle comes out clean.

SPICY HONEY BUTTER
1 stick butter room temperature
1 tablespoon honey
1/2 tin mild green chilies

Mix all together and wrap in clingfilm. Shape into a log and spin ends to seal tightly. Chill and cut into coins to serve.

GARLIC SAUTEED BROCCOLI
4 cups broccoli cut into florets
2 tablespoons extra virgin olive oil
2 tablespoons water
4 cloves garlic sliced thin

Heat olive oil in a large skillet. Add garlic until softened but not browned. Cook broccoli until tender crisp, sprinkle with water.

SALT CRUSTED BABY POTATOES
4 cups baby potatoes
Cold water to barely cover
3 tablespoons pink Himalayan sea salt
1 tablespoon extra-virgin olive oil
2 tablespoons chopped parsley

Boil potatoes in salt water until tender. Water will be almost boiled off. Drain if necessary. Do not add extra water, you want the water to be completely evaporated so the sea salt will create a crust.
Smash lightly. Drizzle with extra-virgin olive oil and sprinkle parsley over top.

CITRUS GREEN BEANS
2 cups green beans topped and tailed
1 orange zested and juiced
Himalayan pink sea salt and freshly cracked pepper to taste

Steam green beans in orange juice until tender crisp. Sprinkle with salt, pepper and orange zest.

Plump and perfect, paired with piquant tomato!!

PISTOU PORTOBELLO
4 Portobello mushrooms cleaned with stumps and gills removed
8 tablespoons pistou
4 thick slices of tomato
Himalayan pink sea salt and freshly cracked pepper to taste

Clean Portobello mushrooms and remove the stumps and gills. I use a teaspoon to scrape the gills out. Spoon 2 tablespoons of pistou into each mushroom, top with one thick slice of tomato. Salt and pepper to taste. Grill on the barbecue or roast in the oven. Mushrooms will fill with an aromatic liquor so careful not to spill!

PISTOU
1/2 cup extra virgin olive oil
1/2 cup basil packed
2 cloves garlic
Himalayan pink sea salt to taste

Whiz everything together in a blender until puréed. Can also be made with parsley, arugula or cilantro!

Carrot Pride - Out Loud and Proud!!
Positive stance against discrimination and violence.
Pride is the predominant outlook that promotes self-affirmation, dignity and equality. Celebrate the diverse and the familiar flavour of our favourite root vegetable. Roasted to enhance their inherent sweetness, this rainbow satisfies.

ROASTED RAINBOW CARROTS
Carrots orange, red, yellow, white and purple
Olive oil
Himalayan pink sea salt
Fresh ground pepper

Scrub carrots clean and cut into large chunks. Massage with oil, Himalayan pink sea salt and freshly cracked pepper to taste. Spread onto cookie sheets. Bake at 375 degrees until al dente. I find these colourful beauties at the farmers market in the middle of summer thru to fall.

Goddesses Mediterranean Feast. Briny salinity, unctuous and creamy. Enticing textural mosaic.

MEDITERRANEAN ROAST VEGETABLES
2 boxes frozen artichoke hearts thawed
5 Roma tomatoes halved
4 cloves garlic minced
1/4 cup capers
1/2 cup Kalamata olives
1 orange juiced
1 orange peel - no pith
1/4 cup white wine
1/4 cup olive oil

Line a large baking sheet with parchment. Gently snuggle tomatoes and artichokes on sheet and strew with capers and olives. Anoint with olive oil, drizzle with wine and spritz orange over all. Tuck in the orange peel. Bake at 425 degrees for 10 - 15 minutes until brown and crispy on the edges.

Add to the feast Crockpot Lemon Potatoes and Greek
Marinated Tofu - heavenly!

CROCKPOT LEMON POTATOES
10 medium russet potatoes peeled and halved
1/4 cup olive oil
2 tablespoons vegan butter
1 lemon juiced and zested
5 cloves garlic minced
1 tablespoon dried oregano
Himalayan pink sea salt and fresh ground pepper to taste
(lots)
1/4 cup fresh parsley chopped to garnish

Toss with abandon into crockpot and cook 2-3 hours on
high or 4-5 hours on low. Garnish with parsley. When you
cook fresh herbs, they tend to go bitter.

Patient and placid, the peaceful potato is personable when paired with its psychedelic playmates. Each is individual as to flavour and texture, but more alike than different.

ROASTED POTATO RAINBOW
Potatoes - lots! cut to similar size
Extra virgin olive oil
Himalayan sea salt and fresh cracked pepper to taste
Fresh minced herbs such as parsley, cilantro, basil, sage, rosemary or chives

Check out specialty produce stores or farmers market for a variety of potatoes. I have found white, yellow, red and purple potatoes, and white potatoes with beige, brown or red skins. Each colour potato is slightly different with some being softer, some are waxy and some are sweeter. They're pleasurable mixed up together drizzled with olive oil, Himalayan sea salt and fresh cracked pepper. Lovingly envelop the humble tubers with your favourite herbs and bake at 350 degrees until tender.

Nutty and sensible, brown rice is all gussied up for the party!

BROWN RICE PILAF
1 tablespoon olive oil
1 small onion chopped
3 cloves garlic minced
1/2 cup carrot diced fine
1/4 cup dried fruit such as cranberries, dried cherries or raisins
2 1/2 cups vegetable broth
1 cup brown rice
Himalayan pink sea salt and cracked pepper
Parsley chopped
Pine nuts chopped

Heat olive oil in a large pot. Sauté onion, carrots, garlic and add rice. Lightly brown the rice and pour in the vegetable stock. Cook according to package directions. Delicately top with pine nuts and parsley.
Soft and savoury, this vegetable dish stands up to hearty barbecue.

DWAYNES VEGETABLE SAUTE
2 tablespoons olive oil
2 large onions sliced
2 cups mushroom sliced
1 large bell pepper sliced
1 cup grape tomatoes
1 lemon juiced
1/2 teaspoon each dried oregano and basil
Himalayan sea salt to taste
Pepper, lots!

Sauté onions in skillet until softened. Add mushrooms and bell pepper. Dump in tomatoes and cook until they start to burst. Add seasonings and lemon juice. Serve and enjoy! This is his go to side for steak, but I like with grilled corn

GARLICKY BOK CHOY
2 tablespoons of EVOO
3 cloves garlic micro-planed or grated
8 cups bok choy chopped bite size
1 small red chili* minced
1/2 teaspoon soy sauce
½ lemon

Heat olive oil in large skillet and add micro planed garlic. Quickly throw in the bok choy and the chili and toss. Sprinkle with soy sauce and spritz with lemon.
*Remove the seeds from your chili for less heat.

ROAST POTATOES
3 cups baby potatoes
¼ cup olive oil
Pink Himalayan sea salt to taste
Fresh cracked pepper to taste
½ cup sour cream
3 spring onions (finely sliced)
Charred lemon

Heat oven to 425 degrees. In a shallow baking dish, topple in the scrubbed baby potatoes. Smother with olive oil, salt and pepper. Roast until blistered and soft. Squeeze lemon over potatoes. Serve with sour cream mixed with onion.

NOTES:

Vicky Gosse

SHOW STOPPERS

SHOW STOPPERS

Showstoppers are the fancy dishes that come out once or twice a year, usually for holidays. Traditionally turkey dinner or an enormous prime rib roast. I have kept the special feel, but make them more inclusive for everyone.

The vegetable accompaniment is usually creamy and rich with little resemblance to how it started out. I have updated some of the classics with fewer mini marshmallow mom short cuts and use a fresher version. There is a reason we only eat like this a couple of times a year and that is because these dishes are a luxury to be savoured occasionally. There is something about tradition that makes the truly awful, cravable. Otherwise, jellied salad would not exist.

Creamy, dreamy, fluffy and comforting. Gild the lily with lashings of ambrosial gravy. A vegan version of the classic.

VEGAN MASHED POTATOES
10 russet potatoes peeled, cut into large chunks
Water to cover
4 large tablespoons of vegetable bouillon paste or powder
3 cloves garlic whole
1 cup vegan cream cheese
1 cup vegan sour cream
3 teaspoons onion powder
Sea salt to taste

Cook potatoes in a large pot of boiling water with vegetable stock and garlic. Drain, keeping your cooking water. Mash or rice potatoes, but don't overwork. While still hot gently stir in cream cheese, sour cream, and onion powder. (Add a little cooking water if potatoes are too thick.) Taste and add salt. Spoon into a large greased casserole dish. You can wrap and freeze for later. Bake 30 minutes at 375. (If frozen, thaw before baking)

VEGAN GRAVY
I confess, I use a prepackaged mix. I jazz it up a little by caramelizing a chopped onion in olive oil and using left over vegetable water and a few glugs of wine, cider or beer. Fresh cracked pepper to taste.

Slightly sweet, slightly nutty - bright and fruity - with a crisply clean finish. Is there anything this ubiquitous vegetable CAN'T do?

CARROTS, GREEN GRAPES AND VODKA
2 lbs. carrots
1/4 cup (vegan) butter
1/4 cup brown sugar
1/4 cup vodka
Himalayan pink sea salt to taste
2 cups seedless green grapes

Peel carrots. I like the look of them whole or sliced lengthwise on the plate. Boil in salted water until tender crisp. Drain carrots (saving water for gravy). Melt butter and add brown sugar. When mixture is melted and bubbly deglaze pan with vodka. Combine gently with carrots and grapes. Keep warm in a covered dish until ready to serve.

The bawdy beet is charmed by a fresh orange vinaigrette.

BEETS WITH ORANGE VINAIGRETTE
12 beets
1/4 cup olive oil
Himalayan Pink Sea Salt and Ground Black Pepper
Remove tops and tails of beets and peel with a vegetable peeler. Cut into quarters. Brush beets with EVOO, salt and pepper. Roast 35 - 40 minutes at 375 degrees until pierces easily with a fork. Dress while still hot.

ORANGE VINAIGRETTE
2 oranges zested and juiced
2 tablespoons red wine vinegar
Himalayan pink sea salt to taste
1/3 cup olive oil
Zest and juice two oranges. Mix all ingredients together and baptize your hot beets.

Stuffing savoury with sage, onion and garlic. Perky parsley freshens with a grassy note of green.

TURKEY-FREE STUFFING
1 large onion diced
4 stalks celery diced
2 cloves garlic minced
1/4 cup olive oil
Himalayan pink sea salt and fresh ground pepper to taste
8 cups dried bread cubes
1 tablespoon poultry seasoning
1 teaspoon each ground sage, onion powder, garlic powder, summer savoury,
2 tablespoons nutritional yeast optional
1 litre vegetarian soup stock
1/2 cup fresh chopped parsley

Sauté onion and celery in olive oil until softened. Add garlic, salt and pepper to taste. Grease casserole dish or crockpot. Combine bread, spices and vegetable mixture. Stir in stock one cup at a time until bread is moistened. Bread should lightly hold together when squeezed. Taste and adjust seasoning and stock. Bake 350 degrees for one hour covered and 1/2 hour uncovered or cook 4-6 hours in crock pot, stirring occasionally. Keep tasting and add salt and pepper and more stock if too dry. If dressing is too moist, cook with lid off. Embellish with lots of parsley!
*Stuffing is one of those dishes that is so subjective. This is very basic but if I stray my family complains! Nuts, raisins, dried fruit, pears or apples are yummy add ins. Change it up with corn bread, cumin and cayenne. I usually advocate for fresh herbs, but when cooked for a while, they become bitter. If you want to use them, add to vegetable sauté for flavour then remove, or chop finely and stir in when stuffing is done. I would add small amounts, separately, and KEEP TASTING.

A tangy, tantalizing accoutrement perfumed with Grand Marnier. Not your usual quivering blob.

CRANBERRY SAUCE
1 cup white sugar
1 cup liquid - water or 1/2 cup orange juice and 1/2 cup water
4 cups cranberries - fresh or frozen - 12 ounce package
2 - 3 tablespoons Grande Marnier or other orange liquor optional

Boil sugar and water, stirring until sugar is melted and boiling hard. Make sure your pot is nice and big. Carefully stir in cranberries and return to a boil. Lower the heat and simmer 10 minutes or so until most of the cranberries have popped. The longer you simmer, the firmer the berries. Spill in the GM and your potion will foam up quite dramatically. Allow a few minutes to burn off the alcohol (or not), and cool for a few hours This keeps a month in a mason jar in the fridge.

NOTES:

INDEX

SANDWICHES

STARTERS

GARLIC SAUTEED BROCCOLI, Pg.103
SIDES CONT.
SALT CRUSTED BABY POTATOES, Pg.103
CITRUS GREEN BEANS, Pg.103
PISTOU PORTOBELLO, Pg.104
ROASTED RAINBOW CARROTS, Pg.105
MEDITERRANEAN ROAST VEGETABLES, Pg.106
CROCKPOT LEMON POTATOES, Pg.107
ROASTED POTATO RAINBOW, Pg.108
BROWN RICE PILAF, Pg.109
DWAYNES VEGETABLE SAUTE, Pg.110
GARLICKY BOK CHOY, Pg.110
ROAST POTATOES, Pg.111

SHOW STOPPERS
VEGAN MASHED POTATOES, Pg.115
    VEGAN GRAVY, Pg.115
CARROTS, GREEN GRAPES AND VODKA, Pg.116
BEETS WITH ORANGE VINAIGRETTE, Pg.117
TURKEY-FREE STUFFING, Pg.118
CRANBERRY SAUCE, Pg.119

ABOUT THE AUTHOR

Vicky Gosse is the author and recipe designer for "The Intuitive Artichoke - A Year of Meatless Mondays".
She is also the Meatless Monday contributor for the 'Yogini's Guide; Intuition Is A Choice Newsletter", and answers the food related questions for "Ask A Yogini". Vicky also cooks vegetarian food for yoga and wellness retreats. Vicky lives in Calgary, Alberta with her husband, Dwayne and they have two children, Zach and Georgia.

PRAISE FOR THE INTUITIVE ARTICHOKE

"I had the incredible good fortune of being treated to the culinary expertise of FOOD GODDESS, VICKY GOSSE, at a weeklong yoga retreat where she served us the most unbelievable vegetarian taste sensations! I grew up on a farm and vegetables were always the "side" to the main...and as a mom with a meat loving husband and sons, vegetables really didn't take center stage...I just hoped they ate some of what I prepared....I wish I had met Vicky sooner, as she certainly takes "boring" and "intimidation" out of the idea of vegetarian cooking ..she always combines such interesting market finds with great herbs and spices - and her dishes have such visual appeal, your mouth just starts to water!! Vicky is an unbelievable talent - with a real passion and flare for creating unique, flavorful recipes. I can't wait to try the recipes in this book and share it with my friends and family!!"
~Lana Lojczyc

"I had the pleasure to meet and spend a week with the lovely Vicky Gosse in Mexico. She was our food goddess & prepared the most delicious vegan meals!...prepare yourselves peeps, for the most scrumptious recipes created with love and care for our souls.
~Heather Neighbour

Vicky is a true inspiration with her vegetarian cooking. I love to try her recipes and they've all been excellent. I served one dish at a dinner party and everyone asked for the recipe (Curried chickpeas and spinach). I am so excited for her book to come out and I will be making good use of it!!! Congratulations to you Vicky on your new book!!!
~Patti Faulkner

Made in the USA
Columbia, SC
02 December 2017